JOHN

C000102929

Discovering
Bells and
Bellringing

SHIRE PUBLICATIONS LTD.

Contents

Photographs are acknowledged as follows: Whitechapel Bell Foundry, plates 1, 2, 3, 4, 5, 6; J. W. Whitelaw, plate 7; Cadbury Lamb, plates 8, 9, 11, 12; Taylor's Bell Foundry, plate 10; Hallam Ashley, plate 13.

Cover picture: 'The Ringers of Launcells' by Frederick Smallfield ARWS (1829-1915). The original painting hangs in the County Museum and Art Gallery, Truro, and is reproduced by permission of the Royal Institution of Cornwall.

Copyright © 1968 and 1988 by John Camp. Number 29 in the Discovering series. First published 1968; reprinted 1971. Second edition 1975; reprinted 1977, 1979, 1981 and 1984. Third edition 1988; reprinted 1992. ISBN 0 85263 913 9.
All rights reserved. No part of this publication may be reproduced or transmitted in any form or by any means, electronic or mechanical, including photocopy, recording, or any information storage and retrieval system, without permission in writing from the publishers, Shire Publications Ltd, Cromwell House, Church Street, Princes Risborough, Buckinghamshire HP27 9AJ, UK.

Printed in Great Britain by C. I. Thomas & Sons (Haverfordwest) Ltd, Press Buildings, Merlins Bridge, Haverfordwest, Dyfed SA61 1XF.

Foreword

To most people, bellringing appears a mysterious and highly complex subject, exceeded in difficulty only by Mah-Jong and practised exclusively by those with an I.Q. well above the average. Ignorance of the subject is gargantuan in its proportions. It is the object of this book to explain as simply as possible the theory and practice of ringing for those who are interested, and, in addition, to sketch briefly the historical and social background to ringing. Few people realise that bellringing, as we are accustomed to hearing it in England, is restricted virtually to this country and is impossible anywhere else. How this came about is explained, as are the reasons why the situation is unlikely to alter. Details are given of notable bells and towers in Britain, and a glossary of ringing terms is included.

Bellringing has the advantage that once a learner has mastered the technique of handling a bell it is up to him how far he becomes involved in the technicalities of the subject. There are many ringers who have never progressed beyond 'rounds' and some, even, have remained happily with 'call-changes'. Others have forged on and plumbed the mysteries of 'surprise' methods and graduated to membership of one of the ancient ringing societies. It is hoped that the following pages will serve to whet the appetite for a closer knowledge of the subject which will lead to a visit to a local belfry and a decision to take up ringing.

If this happens this book will have achieved its main object. But, even if it does not have this result, a little light may be shed on a subject that has a wealth of history and anecdote, has played a surprisingly important part in the social history of England — and, what is more, continues to do so. If only for these reasons it deserves a wider public.

JOHN CAMP   WINGRAVE

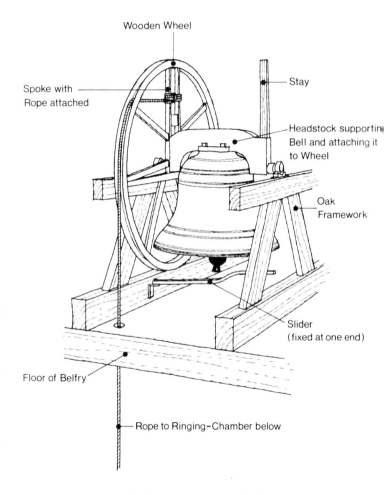

Wooden Wheel

Spoke with
Rope attached

Stay

Headstock supporting
Bell and attaching it
to Wheel

Oak
Framework

Slider
(fixed at one end)

Floor of Belfry

Rope to Ringing-Chamber below

Bell hung for change-ringing.

1. The background to bellringing

'If all the bells in England were rung at one time . . .' remarked Bishop Latimer, in 1552, '. . . there would scarcely be a single spot where a bell would not be heard'. Though the bishop was referring to the ease with which the population could be warned in the event of an invasion from the sea, it is also a comment on the number of churches with bells that had existed in pre-Reformation England.

Although bells have occasionally been used to signal disaster, in most countries they are more intimately associated with churches and places of worship. The history of bells as a means of communication, both religious and secular, goes back into the mists of time and is a study in itself. This book deals with church bells in England and it attempts to explain why ringing, as practised in this country, is peculiar to Britain and is practically unknown elsewhere.

Early methods of hanging bells

Up to the fourteenth century church bells, here and abroad, were normally hung on a simple spindle and chimed by pulling a rope attached to the spindle. But about that time ringers began to experiment with new ways of hanging the bell so that greater control could be exercised over it. The first improvement was made by mounting the bell, not directly on to a spindle, but to a wooden quarter-wheel, the spindle serving as the axle with the rope attached to the rim of the wheel. As this system gradually came into use a further step evolved by mounting the bell on a half wheel, which allowed even more control. This was the situation in most churches and monasteries up to the reign of Henry VIII. Most parish churches had two or three bells, while the larger churches and monastic establishments had eight or even ten.

One result of the Reformation was the desecration of monastic buildings and abbeys throughout the land which involved the destruction of much church property and the silencing or even the removal of many church bells. When the smoke of battle, still smelling faintly of incense, had finally cleared, the lengthy task of restoration and repair began, a job which, in many cases, necessitated re-hanging the bells.

Developments after the Reformation

But the lessons learned from the quarter and half-wheel had not been forgotten. The opportunity was now present to complete the experiment by using the whole wheel, and it was in this manner that most bells were eventually re-hung. Although, from this point on, a greater degree of control was possible, and the swing of the bell could be slowed down or speeded up with the help of the rope,

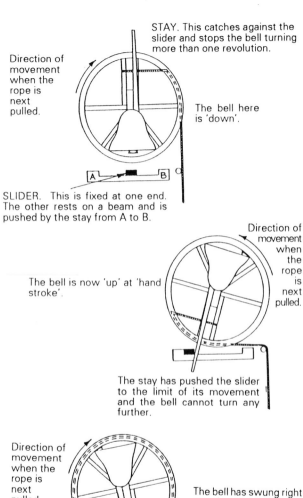

STAY. This catches against the slider and stops the bell turning more than one revolution.

Direction of movement when the rope is next pulled.

The bell here is 'down'.

SLIDER. This is fixed at one end. The other rests on a beam and is pushed by the stay from A to B.

Direction of movement when the rope is next pulled.

The bell is now 'up' at 'hand stroke'.

The stay has pushed the slider to the limit of its movement and the bell cannot turn any further.

Direction of movement when the rope is next pulled.

The bell has swung right round and is now 'up' at 'back stroke'.

The bellringing cycle.

there was still no way by which the bell's movement could be halted at will or restarted equally quickly. The final refinement of the slider and the stay at last made this possible. By pulling harder on the rope as the bell swung upwards the ringer could check it as it reached its upside-down position and ease it gently off balance, resting against the slider, where it would remain until required to sound again. This is known as 'setting' the bell, and it is the use of this technique that paved the way for the development of change-ringing in England.

Oddly enough, despite the successful experiments which led to the adoption of the whole wheel in England, the practice did not find favour abroad, and only in Belgium did a few towers re-hang their bells this way. Even so they did not bother with the slider and stay, but eventually moved towards purely mechanical methods of ringing resulting in the many fine carillons found throughout the country. Controlled ringing, therefore, remained restricted to Britain, and virtually to England, as it was confined to 'established' churches. Non-conformist chapels usually had only one bell, and for over three hundred years Roman Catholic churches were forbidden to have any bells at all.

The cost of maintaining the bells and equipment, together with payments to ringers, could be quite a high proportion of the running expenses of the parish. It is fortunate that there are many churchwardens' accounts still in existence by which we can trace the repairs and alterations made over the years. It is also interesting to note the relative importance accorded to events signalled by ringing the bells, and the payment made to the ringers. In 1586, for instance, the churchwardens of St. Margaret's, Westminster, paid the ringers one shilling each ' . . . for ringing at the beheading of the Queen of Scotts'. Less than twenty years later the same ringers were paid ten times that sum for ringing ' . . . at the time when the Parliament House should have been blown up'. Before the Reformation ringing in cathedrals and monasteries was normally the duty of deacons. With the introduction of the whole wheel and the gradual evolution of change-ringing more and more of the laity interested themselves in the art and gradually took over the belfry from the clerics. Extra bells were installed in many towers.

Ringing societies

There is nothing the average Englishman likes better than joining an association. It was therefore inevitable that before long societies of lay-ringers should be formed, and from the early 1600s these were established up and down the country. Most of them have long since ceased to exist, but one or two still survive and are justifiably proud of their tradition. One such is the Ancient Society of College Youths, founded in 1637, whose members normally provide the ringing at St. Paul's Cathedral and Westminster Abbey. The 'College' of the title was the College of the Holy Ghost, founded in the City of London by the Lord Mayor, Dick Whittington, in 1424. The College Youths, together with the Royal Society of Cumberland Youths formed in 1747, represent the elite of the ringing world. Membership is by invitation only, after introduction by a member, and then only if the candidate's ringing ability reaches the required standard. Ringing on state occasions at Westminster Abbey or St Paul's does not allow for any mistakes!

Few ringers aspire to this standard of proficiency and most are content to contribute their regular quota to Sunday ringing in their parish church; for, when all is said and done, calling the faithful to prayer is the main object of ringing. The fact that it is, in addition, an extremely interesting and rewarding hobby should never be allowed to obscure its prime function. Today regular ringing goes on in nearly 6,000 churches up and down the country. Present-day ringers are encouraged to join the diocesan guild of their particular church, or their county association, and *The Ringing World*, the weekly journal of the Central Council of Church Bellringers records peal and quarter-peal successes and prints general news and features dealing with bells and ringers everywhere. In addition there are very many ringers' associations within certain professions or communities. Most universities, for instance, have their own ringing association, and a Police Ringing Guild exists as well as one whose members are all railwaymen. There is also a Guild of Medical Ringers. Many girls have become ringers during the past few years as, contrary to popular belief, ringing does not call for a great deal of physical effort: today most bells are mounted with ball bearings and swing very easily. To be a success a ringer requires an orderly mind, a memory that is retentive and capable of classification and a good sense of timing. Why these characteristics are so important is explained in the next few pages.

2. The technique of ringing

The adoption of the whole wheel made it possible for ringers to vary the order in which the bells rang. Ringing in order from the lightest bell (the treble) down to the heaviest (the tenor) in descending scale, is ringing 'rounds'. The bells are numbered from 1 (treble) to tenor. To vary the ringing the captain may, during rounds, call out the number of two adjacent bells, upon which these two bells change places in the order of ringing by the simple expedient of one ringer speeding his bell and the other retarding his. They continue to ring in this new order until another 'change' is called, and a whole series of different changes may be rung until the bells are finally 'called' back to ringing in rounds. Call-changes are a popular method of ringing and indeed, form the lower slopes of the new ringer's tuition. But, in addition, call-changes sound musical to the outside ear especially if each is repeated long enough for its arrangement to be appreciated before the next change is called. In Cornwall and the West Country call-changes are by far the most popular form of ringing, and even rounds, assuming the striking is good, can be a delight to listen to and are far from tedious. The term 'striking' in this context means the ability to ring so that there is a regular and unvarying interval between the sound of each bell. Striking should be unhurried to be effective, and the deep-toned tenor bell, usually ringing last, sets the pace and, in a way, beats time for the other bells.

Stedman and the 'method'

Though call-changes were progressively popular from the early seventeenth century it was some years before the full possibilities of this type of ringing became apparent. Whilst the West Country continued perfecting the technique of call-changes, at the other end of England a Cambridge printer, Fabian Stedman, was absorbed in the mathematics of the variations possible on a given number of bells. The order of ringing of three bells could be changed six times without repetition ($3 \times 2 \times 1$) and the variations possible on four bells amounted to twenty-four ($4 \times 3 \times 2 \times 1$). But the majority of churches had more than four bells, and when the possible number of changes was calculated the results were surprising. On six bells the number was 720, while eight bells could be varied 40,320 ways! When the number of changes possible on twelve bells was calculated it was found to run into millions, further calculations demonstrating that to ring every one of them would take a band of ringers nearly thirty years!

Stedman, who was an early member of the College Youths, wrote the first book on ringing in 1668. In this, and in his second book *Campanologia*, published nine years later, he describes the art of ringing and draws up rules or procedures which enable long series of changes to be rung without the need for anyone to 'call'. There was no longer any time allowed between changes, the bells changing places at each pull of the rope. As a result of Stedman's groundwork, and with the addition of further rules evolved soon afterwards, a whole series of changes could be worked out in advance, written down and learned by heart. Such a series was termed a 'method', and each method was given a name, many of which are still in use. It was also decided that 5,000 or more changes should be called a 'peal', and anything less than this a 'touch'. It is therefore incorrect to refer to a church as having a 'peal' of bells, as this refers to the number of changes being rung. The number of bells in a church is referred to as a 'ring'. Most churches in England have a ring of six or eight bells.

Names of towns and cities where they were first rung were often given to methods, and *Norwich, London* and *Cambridge* are rung today together with scores of other methods like *Grandsire* (pronounced as if there were no final 'e') and *Stedman,* named after the 'father' of ringing. It was also necessary to say how many bells were used in a method, and another word to indicate this had to be added. The name given to methods rung on five bells, for instance, is Doubles; on six bells, Minor; on seven bells, Triples; on eight bells, Major; and so on to Maximus on twelve bells.

Thus *Grandsire* on five bells is called *Grandsire Doubles,* and, if rung on seven bells, *Grandsire Triples.*

Doubles and Triples

Doubles and Triples are very popular with ringers, and remembering that these are five- and seven-bell methods, and that most churches have six or eight bells, this might, at first sight, appear odd. The explanation is that Doubles rung with six bells allows the tenor to ring last each time, as it does not take part in the method. This has the effect not only of marking a steady rhythm but also of dividing up the ringing into definite sections ending on the same note rather like the rhyme in a poem, and is thus more satisfying to listen to. By far the best way to understand what happens in method-ringing is to write out the first few changes of a method, and then to mark the path of one particular bell to see what 'work' it does. Let us, therefore, write out the beginning of *Grandsire Doubles,* and mark (or 'prick out') the path of bell No. 5. We shall assume this is in a six-bell tower, with the tenor bell ringing 'behind' at each stroke. If we do the same with another method, for example *Stedman Doubles,* the contrast between the work of the bell in the two methods becomes apparent.

N.B. Only five bells are changing places, the tenor
ringing last each time.

GRANDSIRE DOUBLES

```
1 2 3 4 5 6
2 1 3 5 4 6
2 3 1 4 5 6
3 2 4 1 5 6
3 4 2 5 1 6
4 3 5 2 1 6
4 5 3 1 2 6
5 4 1 3 2 6
5 1 4 2 3 6
1 5 2 4 3 6
1 2 5 3 4 6
2 1 5 4 3 6
2 5 1 3 4 6
5 2 3 1 4 6
5 3 2 4 1 6
3 5 4 2 1 6
3 4 5 1 2 6
4 3 1 5 2 6
4 1 3 2 5 6
1 4 2 3 5 6
1 2 4 5 3 6
2 1 4 3 5 6
2 4 1 5 3 6
4 2 5 1 3 6
4 5 2 3 1 6
5 4 3 2 1 6
5 3 4 1 2 6
3 5 1 4 2 6
3 1 5 2 4 6
1 3 2 5 4 6
          etc.
```

STEDMAN DOUBLES

```
1 2 3 4 5 6
2 1 3 5 4 6
2 3 1 4 5 6
3 2 4 1 5 6
2 3 4 5 1 6
2 4 3 1 5 6
4 2 3 5 1 6
4 3 2 1 5 6
3 4 2 5 1 6
4 3 5 2 1 6
4 5 3 1 2 6
5 4 3 2 1 6
5 3 4 1 2 6
3 5 4 2 1 6
3 4 5 1 2 6
4 3 1 5 2 6
3 4 1 2 5 6
3 1 4 5 2 6
1 3 4 2 5 6
1 4 3 5 2 6
4 1 3 2 5 6
1 4 2 5 3 6
1 2 4 5 3 6
2 1 4 3 5 6
2 4 1 5 3 6
4 2 1 3 5 6
4 1 2 5 3 6
1 4 5 2 3 6
4 1 5 3 2 6
4 5 1 2 3 6
          etc.
```

*Order of ringing for bell
No. 5 in first thirty
changes.*

The work of any bell in the method can be isolated and studied
in this way.

Though the bells change places in a different pattern in each
method, they do so while conforming to certain basic rules.

Dodging and hunting

Special terms are used to denote the various manoeuvres
performed by the bell. In *Grandsire,* for instance, No. 5 bell begins
by changing places with No. 4 bell, but then changes back. This is
known as dodging. Having done this, No. 5 then speeds up
its stroke so that its turn comes earlier and earlier until at length it

is the first bell to ring in the sequence. In *Grandsire*, when any bell reaches this position of leading, it rings twice in that place, before beginning to work its way back until it is once again the last bell to ring. Here again we see the value of the tenor bell ringing sixth all the time, as when No. 5 gets to the position of ringing first, he knows that he must ring immediately *after* the tenor, who was the last to ring in the change immediately before. The manoeuvre of the bell gradually changing from being the first one to ring to being the last is called 'hunting up'. The reverse procedure, from ringing last to ringing first, is 'hunting down'. A cardinal rule of ringing that is so taken for granted that beginners are rarely told of it is that a bell can only change places with the bell that is ringing next to it, i.e. either before it or after it. In the second change of *Grandsire*, No. 5 can change only with No. 3 or No. 4. It cannot change places with No. 1 (the treble) or with bell No. 2.

Though, at first sight, these rules and expressions may seem complicated, it is only because of them that ringers can memorise long sequences of changes. A full peal of over 5,000 changes takes a little over three hours on most bells. To a non-ringer it seems incredible that anyone should be able to ring a bell for that length of time, non-stop, and at each pull ensure that his bell is ringing in its correct order in relation to the others. But once a ringer has mastered the work in a particular method it is merely a question of repeating that pattern again and again for as long as is required to ring the full peal. The fact that the pattern of one bell's path is repeated several times during a peal does not necessarily mean that any of the actual changes are repeated, because each bell is at a different stage in its work. In addition, should the next change in the series be a repetition of one already rung, then a 'dodge' or similar procedure is introduced to avoid this happening.

Ringing in the belfry

So far we have dealt with a simplified account of the theory behind method ringing. To put it into practice in the belfry is a very different matter.

For a start, and to be strictly accurate, it is not done in the belfry, but in the ringing-chamber. The belfry is the room or part of the tower in which the bells themselves are hung. The bells are of different sizes, have different-size wheels, and are mounted in such a way that some swing in one direction and some another. This is done to cancel out the strain that would be imposed on the tower if all the bells swung in the same plane, just as marchers break step when crossing a temporary or lightweight bridge. The bells are mounted in a frame of wood or metal.

The rope that runs round the perimeter of the wheel goes down into the ringing-chamber through a hole in the ceiling. A few feet before its end each rope includes a section of fluffy thick material

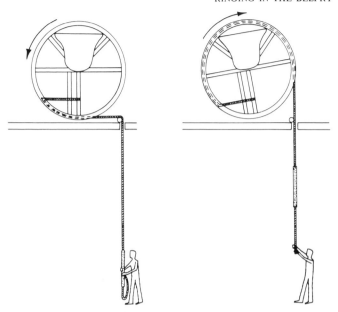

*The position of the bellrope at hand-stroke (left)
and back-stroke (right).*

about three feet long and with green or red, white and blue stripes. This is the sally, and is a very useful item in learning method ringing.

The rope itself is attached to one of the spokes from where it goes through a hole on to the rim. The rim is trough-shaped and the tension of the rope while ringing keeps it in position as the wheel swings backwards and forwards. As will be seen from the accompanying diagram the swing of the wheel one way allows the maximum amount of rope to hang down into the ringing chamber, and this is called 'hand-stroke'. As the bell swings back and up the other way the rope has to extend a greater distance before going down and the length available is correspondingly less. This is the 'back-stroke'. In ringing, therefore, each pull on the rope leads either to hand-stroke or back-stroke, the result being that on one stroke there is a surplus amount of rope which loops down to the floor and up to the ringer's hand, while at the next stroke the end of the rope is just above his head. The rope can be adjusted to suit the individual requirements of either a very short or very tall person.

Rope-sight

In some towers the belfry is just above the ringing-chamber, and a pull on the rope has an almost instantaneous effect on the bell. In other towers the ringers may find they are at ground-level, with the bells at the top of a very tall tower. The distance between bells and ringers is called the 'draught', and a tower may have a long or short draught. One of the many complications of ringing is the fact that the longer the draught the longer is the interval of time between pulling the rope and the actual movement of the bell, which in any case has to swing through a section of its arc before the clapper hits the side and the bell sounds. This being so, it is no good listening for the bell that strikes before your own, as you will most likely need to start pulling on your rope *before* the previous bell has sounded. This is where the sally comes into its own, and why a good ringer must develop what is called 'rope-sight' at an early stage. If you watch the sallies moving up and down as their bells swing back and forth you will eventually be able to see a relationship between the position of the sallies and the sound of their respective bells. By careful listening for instance you will discover that if you want your bell to ring before bell No. 4 it is necessary for your sally to be just that much in front of No. 4's sally on the way down. Similarly, when ringing after another bell, your sally must be travelling a certain distance behind the other bell's. The exact difference in the relative position of each sally varies with each bell, because each wheel is a different size. Only by constant practice, by watching the movement of the sally and by *listening to your bell* can you ensure that the striking is regular and even. The art of determining just when to pull on your rope by looking at the other ringer's sally is rope-sight. It is worth devoting a good deal of time to this, as in ringing looking is as important as listening.

As a learner, your first task will be to practise handling your bell. For beginners the lightest bell, the treble, is usually used, and to avoid the cacophony produced during this process, the clapper of the bell is fixed, and the bell is rung 'silent'. Once the feel of the bell has been acquired, and it can be controlled with reasonable proficiency, the clapper is freed and the learner allowed to ring normally. By this time he has usually developed a sense of balance and, in addition, a certain amount of complacency. This feeling is quickly destroyed the first time he rings on an 'open' bell with the clapper free. To his consternation he discovers that the 'feel' of the bell is completely different from when the clapper was tied, and again he has difficulty in controlling it. This is because the weight of the clapper, swinging free, affects the swing of the bell first one way then the other. But, with a good teacher, confidence is soon restored, and it is not long before the new ringer is taking his place in ringing rounds, though, for the first few occasions, with an experienced ringer standing behind him to give him any necessary instructions and to take the rope if things get out of control.

From rounds, progress is normally made via call-changes to *Grandsire* and various other methods, and from the treble the learner slowly graduates to the heavier bells.

Bell-ringing has been described as the most democratic of all hobbies. Whether or not this is true is debatable, but it certainly requires a great deal of team-spirit and the ability to work in close relationship with others. The captain of the band may be the local postman, the most junior member the mayor, or the chairman of the parish council. Seniority in the tower is determined solely by ability and experience. In some towers the parish priest is a keen ringer and appears on practice nights, even if he is unable to be in two places at once and to take part in service ringing. The relationship between ringers and clergy is usually an amicable one these days. But a hundred years ago the situation was very different, and open warfare existed in many towers.

Bell stamp of Roger Landen, Wokingham Bell Foundry (fifteenth century).

3. Ringers v. clergy

It has been said that to be a ringer in eighteenth-century England was to be a layabout and a drunk. This is an exaggerated view, but the standards of behaviour were indeed low. The Commonwealth had discouraged ringing, and from the early 1700s the clergy had virtually vacated the belfry, and ringing was carried out by locals who, in most cases, saw an easy opportunity for earning an extra shilling or two. Ringing being thirsty work, the additional income transferred itself with remarkable speed from the church tower to the village inn. In town, mainly because of the higher standards of ringing imposed by the various societies and guilds, the situation did not deteriorate to such an extent. Again, because of the denser population near the church, ringing in town was restricted mainly to church feasts and service-ringing, and only the most important secular occasions were commemorated with the bells.

But in the rural areas any and every opportunity was taken to ring. Those who rang did so mainly as a hobby and usually for gain—attendance at church services was considered no part of bellringing! The arrival of the mail-coach from London was often signalled by the bells, or the squire's birthday celebrated in similar fashion. The village fair was always started off with a spell of ringing, and what with the never-ending series of births, marriages and deaths in the community the ringers were rarely at a loss for an excuse to perform, for which the tavern-keepers were duly grateful. The standard of behaviour in most belfries became appalling. Cursing, swearing and smoking were normal, and in many towers a barrel of beer was always 'on tap' in the ringing-chamber. But this must be viewed in the light of prevailing custom, and was not as scandalous as some writers infer.

Beer was the normal drink of most people in days when the water-supply was anything but safe and tea and coffee were only for the well-to-do. The Temperance Movement originated in the efforts of brewers to get people to drink beer rather than the pernicious gin that caused such havoc, and, in its early days, the movement did not advocate total abstinence. Beer drinking was taken for granted, as shown by a charmingly candid entry in the parish accounts of a church in Lancashire: 'Spent on ourselves when we met at the Abbey Arms to decide how much to give to the Society for the Propagation of the Gospel.'

Occasions for bellringing

In many parishes the original use of the bells to signal the Angelus or Compline became adapted to secular purposes and in others new uses for the bells were found. In Louth, Lincolnshire, bells signalled the beginning of harvesting, and a Harvest Home

1. *In the belfry: the bells raised, or 'set'*
preparatory to ringing.

2. *In the belfry: the bells in action.*

3. This bell is down; the wooden stay sticks up.
The rope can clearly be seen in the groove around
the wheel, leading to the ringing chamber below.

4. Now the bell is set at hand-stroke. The stay presses against the pivoting slider. From this position every pull at the rope turns the bell through a full circle first one way, then the other.

5. Bells are cast by pouring molten metal into a mould. Here the cope, or outer part of the mould, is lowered over the core, which shapes the inside of the bell.

6.   Casting the bell. An alloy of 77 per cent copper and 23 per cent tin is used.

7.   Bells made at the Whitechapel Bell Foundry hanging in the church at Aylsham, Norfolk.

8.   At East Bergholt, Suffolk, the church bells are housed in a bell cage in the churchyard.

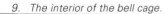

9.   The interior of the bell cage.

10. (Above left) The campanile at Taylor's Bell
Foundry, Loughborough, Leicestershire, has a ring of
ten bells.
11. (Above right) Tom Tower at Christ Church, Oxford,
contains the chiming bell 'Great Tom', which
weighs 147 cwt.

THE CLAPPERS OF THE OLD RING.

OUR DUTY DONE IN BELFRY HIGH,

NOW VOICELESS TONGUES AT REST WE LIE.

PRESERVED BY EDWARD ARCHER ? 887

12.   Clappers from old bells are preserved at Malvern Priory Church, Worcestershire.

13.   The Ringers' Rules at the church of St. Peter Mancroft, Norwich, Norfolk, are written on parchment and date from 1716.

Bell announced the safe arrival of the last load. Private individuals often left bequests for ringing to be carried out on special anniversaries. In several parishes, notably Wokingham, Berkshire, and Wingrave, Buckinghamshire, travellers who were lost and who claimed to have been guided safely home by the bells donated sums for ringing to commemorate the happy event. But of the many private bequests for ringing to give thanks for timely rescue from peril, surely the most cynical is that of Thomas Nashe of Bath. In 1813 this unhappy man left £50 to the Abbey ringers on condition that they rang a peal with bells muffled 'and with solemn and doleful changes' on 14th May, this being the anniversary of his wedding, and on the day of his death to ring 'a grand Bob Major and merry mirthful peals unmuffled in commemoration of my happy release from Domestic tyranny and wretchedness'. The connection between ringing and religion was becoming more and more tenuous. In the light of this situation it is not surprising that before long a deep rift developed between ringers and clergy, amounting, in some parishes, to open hostility. In Devon, for example, the Rector of Mortehoe was locked out of the church tower by the ringers, who then changed the lock on the door, and more than one nervous cleric refused a good living on discovering what sort of ringers controlled the tower.

Even in towns, where ringers were usually more tractable than in the country, they were still extremely independent and often reserved the right to decide when to ring and when not to. At High Wycombe in 1832 the bells were rung to celebrate the passing of the Reform Bill. But a few days later, on the occasion of the annual visit of the Bishop of Lincoln,* the ringers refused to turn out and the bells remained silent as a mark of their disapproval at his having voted against the Bill in the House of Lords.

Although both bells and tower were part of the church fabric and therefore under the authority of the clergy, there was little a parish priest could do against a difficult band of ringers. True, the Law was on his side, and in theory he could take the ringers to court for misusing church property. In a few cases this actually happened, and at Thurnby, in Leicestershire, after legal action by the rector, the ringers were fined and, on refusing to pay, were sentenced to prison where they languished for several weeks until the fine was eventually paid for them—by the rector! But in the closely knit communities of rural England such action by the clergy tended to rebound on itself, resulting in dwindling congregations and a drastic reduction in the collection-money. Most villagers were related to each other, however slightly, and, as so often happens in large families, though relations may criticise each other as much as they wish, criticism from outside the family

*High Wycombe was in the diocese of Lincoln at the time.

results in an immediate call-to-arms and a display of unity as impressive as it is unexpected. But help was at hand, and from an unexpected source. It came from the university city of Oxford, where John Henry Newman and his friends were establishing a school of thought that was later to become the Oxford Movement, and which would eventually exert a profound influence not only on the ritual of the Church of England but also on church architecture and on the future of ringing.

Victorian reform

The wave of Anglo-Catholicism which followed Keble's Oxford Assize sermon of 1833 resulted in the Church of England taking a new look at itself—and at its church buildings. Many did not like what they saw. A reaction against the simplified form of service that had been observed since the Reformation was coupled with a determination to bring more colour and light into the churches, and to create a new concept of the church as a temple of worship rather than merely as a place of prayer. In 1839 the Cambridge Camden Society was formed and from then until 1868 supervised and inaugurated the 'spring-cleaning' of churches throughout the country, while employing architects like Street and Butterfield on the building of new churches in the revived Gothic style that is seen to perfection in such splendid monsters as All Saints, Margaret Street, and Keble College Chapel, Oxford.

But it was Street who was mainly responsible for the restoration of the parish churches. The examination inevitably included the tower and the bells, and even the ringers themselves found they were under close scrutiny. This time the clergy had no doubts about who was in charge, though for the next thirty years and more some ringers were still fighting a rear-guard action to preserve their so-called privileges and rights. Unfortunately there was an over-abundance of enthusiasm to begin with, the result being the loss or destruction of much that was worth preserving. Street and other architects associated with the Camden Society may be said to have completed the work begun three hundred years earlier at the Dissolution of the Monasteries and continued by Cromwell.

But as far as the bells were concerned they could only benefit from the new regime. The antagonism between ringers and clergy was a vicious circle which gave the clergy no cause to spend church funds on the maintenance of bells or belfry. The ringers, in turn, used this fact as proof that the clergy had no interest in ringing, and therefore no business in the tower. The alterations carried out in many churches during the next thirty years were designed to bring ringing back into the ambit of church activity, to improve the standard of ringing and, above all, to ensure proper and reverent behaviour in the ringing-chamber and encourage ringers to attend divine service. The most drastic means of achieving the first of these aims was to lengthen the bell ropes so that they came down to the floor of the tower, and to take out the floor of the ringing-chamber. This resulted in the ringers having to ring in full view of the congregation, and in a noticeable improvement in their standards of behaviour. In addition, the Camden Society (which later changed its name to the Ecclesiological Society) sent representatives round the country talking to ringers about their problems, and trying to find a solution. They encouraged the appointment of tower-captains to decide not only what was to be rung but also to be responsible for regular attendance and for the general conduct of the ringers. Advice was given on the formulation of rules which not only imposed penalties for bad ringing, but also for bad behaviour. The older ringers grumbled—and went on grumbling for a very long time. Typically, they did not give up ringing, but tried to oppose the new system in every possible way. As late as 1865 *The Ecclesiologist* (the journal of the Camden Society) could still print an article by a country curate on the best methods of dealing with 'an ungodly set of ringers'. But the old ways were doomed, and as a new generation of ringers grew up so ringing became respectable and again part of the church. Another reason for the rise in standards was the improvement made to the bells themselves during the restoration process. In many towers they had been re-hung with ball-bearings, or iron frames had taken the place of the old oak frames in the belfry. As a result the bells were much easier to handle, and more complicated methods than before could be tackled—methods that called for a degree of concentration quite impossible with a brain fuddled with alcohol.

By the end of the century women had arrived in the belfry, and the first lady ringer to take part in a complete peal was Miss Alice White, at Basingstoke in 1896. Despite the inevitable opposition from the die-hards, more and more women became interested in ringing, resulting in the eventual formation of the Ladies Guild in 1912. That many men were in favour of lady ringers is shown by the following couplet written at the turn of the century:

Like a breath of summer laden, like a cheery ray of hope,
Is the sight of gentle maiden, deftly handling of a rope.

Problems of the twentieth century

The disillusion which came with the end of World War I and the non-arrival of the Utopia promised by the politicians manifested itself in many ways. Not the least was the swing against organised religion which resulted in a serious decline in church-going and a corresponding reduction in the number of ringers. The most accomplished and well-known personalities continued to ring their peals, duly recorded in the pages of *The Ringing World,* but new ringers were difficult to find and, when found, were likely to be frightened off by the technical talk and self-conscious superiority of many who were supposed to teach them.

The complete stoppage of ringing during World War II had the effect of reviving interest in the art once peace had returned, and from 1950 onwards there has been a steadily increasing flow of recruits to most towers, with a high proportion of girls amongst the learners. But there is still a long way to go, and there are many problems to overcome before every church has enough trained ringers to ensure regular Sunday service ringing and to cope with weddings and other special occasions.

One problem is connected with the educational system. Girls and boys who take up ringing at fourteen or fifteen are usually enthusiastic and attend regularly. Just at the age when they have become proficient enough to make a significant contribution to the band they leave, probably to go to university, and the tower sees them no more. But an even more serious problem is still the attitude of some of the clergy to their ringers. Instead of taking an interest in them, and making them feel they are performing an essential service for the church, some clerics completely ignore the ringers, never visit the ringing-chamber, and are often woefully ignorant which of their congregation are in the band. At Christmas or at Easter, when those who have assisted in decorating the church or who have helped in other ways are publicly thanked in print or from the pulpit, it is rare that any mention is made of the ringers. They are the faceless few who ring Sunday after Sunday and whose presence is noted only on the occasions when they fail to oblige! At certain festivals when it is customary for the various societies connected with the church to be represented in turn, such as the reading of the Lessons at Christmas, one waits in vain for the representative of the ringers.

It would be unfair to imply that this situation exists in all churches. In many of them one may (to paraphrase the old joke) 'find the captain of the ringers hanging in the church porch'. His name is recorded in the parish magazine and might even be on the notice-board in the churchyard.

4. The writing on the wall

(Peal-boards, Ringers' Rules and other graffiti)

The first invented method of change-ringing in accordance with the rules which apply today is called *Plain Bob* and was first rung at Norwich in 1715 as part of the first full peal ever rung. The first peal of Grandsire Triples was also rung here in 1715. Since that time many thousands of methods of different complexity have been rung in towers up and down the country, and the first successful peal in a new method is often commemorated in a board fixed to the chamber wall, and listing the ringers who took part. Almost every parish church has at least one or two peal-boards in the ringing-chamber, and one of the oldest examples was that in St. Bride's, Fleet Street, London, recording the first complete peal of 5,060 *Grandsire Cinques* on 19th January 1724, which was rung by members of the Ancient Society of College Youths. Another early board is to be found at Hillingdon, Greater London, which records the ringing of a peal of 5,040 *Grandsire Triples* by a local band in August 1733. Commenting on this feat the *Penny London Post,* dated 19th August 1733 says: *Last week the young ringers of Hillingdon, near Uxbridge, rang the whole peal of Grandsire Trebles, being 5,040 changes in 3 hours and about 8 minutes, to the great satisfaction of all that heard them.* Occasionally one meets a peal commemorated, not on a board, but in a stained-glass window. One example is at Ripon Cathedral where a window in the belfry gives details of a peal of *Kent Treble Bob Major* rung on 28th August 1886 as part of the celebrations connected with the thousandth anniversary of the city's charter. A more modern window on the same subject is that in the ringing chamber of St. Peter's Church, St. Albans, showing some of the band, and the bells above them, ringing a 'Victory' peal of 5,056 *Plain Bob* in August 1945. Even more interesting is the fact that this window was designed by Martin Webb, himself a ringer at St. Peter's. Though it does not record a peal, there is a very fine window in St. Margaret's, Leicester, in memory of Ernest Morris, author, ringer and historian, who died in 1962. This window also shows various stages in ringing, and the inclusion of fonts, horse brasses and door-knockers in the design is a reference to the wide range of subjects on which Mr. Morris was an authority.

But though most peals are recorded on boards rather than in stained-glass, belfry-boards do not limit themselves to commemorating feats of ringing only. In view of the fact that some ringers do not find it necessary to attend divine worship, a board in the ringing-gallery at St. George's, Littleport, Cambridgeshire, is particularly pertinent:

> *Do not ring and run away*
> *Leaving other folk to pray*

—a sentiment that could well be stressed in many ringing-chambers.

Ringers' Rules

Most old boards found in towers either record peals rung in the past, or list rules for ringing and general behaviour. Unfortunately, many of them were discarded in mid-Victorian times, and others are difficult to decipher. The church of St. Peter Mancroft, Norwich, displays a very fine example of early 'Ringers' Rules' written on a large sheet of parchment and dating from 1716. It is on view near the font, in the north-west corner of the church, and is headed 'Articles of the Association of Bellringers' with illustrations of the three great ringing towers of Norwich, St. Peter Mancroft, St. Giles and St. George, Colegate. All Saints Church, Binfield, Berkshire, where the ringing chamber is at ground level, has a very well-preserved and legible board of 'Ringers Rules' dating from the 1820s when the original five bells were increased to six.

Although most nineteenth-century Ringer's Rules were aimed at improving behaviour among the ringers, there were many regulations and instructions concerned with ringing long before then. Most of these contain a rule about not wearing a hat in the ringing-chamber, and a high proportion also list the penalty for having spurs! The parish church at Bowdon, Greater Manchester, lays down rules in rhyme for the benefit of ringers:

> *You ringers all observe these orders well:*
> *He pays his sixpence who o'erturns his bell;*
> *And he that rings with either Spur or Hat*
> *Must pay his sixpence certainly for that;*
> *And he that rings and does disturbe the peal*
> *Must pay his sixpence or a Gun of Ale.*
> *These laws elsewhere in every church are used*
> *That Bells and Ringers may not be abused.*

At Drewsteignton, a village on Dartmoor, the church also has the rules in verse which, to make sure there is no misunderstanding in the matter, end with these lines:

> *Who will not to these rules agree*
> *Shall not belong to this belfrie.*
> John Hole, Warden.

Bell inscriptions

Most bells are cast with an inscription, usually around the rim. The oldest bells carry the initials and mark of the bell-founder and form a useful guide to the now-vanished bell-foundries that once existed as family businesses throughout the country. One of the oldest and best-known foundries casting bells in the south of England was the Wokingham foundry, known to have been in operation in about 1400. The owner, in 1448, was Roger Landen whose initials, with the letter W for Wokingham and a design of a bell, form his trade-mark and can still be found in a few towers between Surrey and Somerset. By the year 1500 the Wokingham foundry had closed and the work was being carried on by the foundry at Reading, seven miles away. It is pleasant to think that even after five hundred years, Wokingham's foundry is still remembered in the name of a lane in the town.

Only two bell-foundries survive today. The oldest, with a remarkable record of continuity, is the Whitechapel Bell Foundry established in 1570 and still in business in the Whitechapel Road after four centuries! The other foundry is that of John Taylor & Co. in Loughborough, which has been in the hands of the Taylor family since 1786.

The eighteenth century, we have seen, was a time of intense activity in ringing, and many churches with only a few bells had the number increased so that more change-ringing could be practised. The cost of many of these bells was borne by wealthy parishioners who, by stipulating the inscription on the bell, ensured their name would endure at least as long as the tower was standing, if not longer. It became the fashion for these inscriptions to be in English, rather than in Latin, to obtain what today is termed 'maximum readership', though the standard of versification tended to suffer. There is little subtlety or poetry in this inscription of 1700:

> *All you of Bath that hear me sound*
> *Thank Lady Hopton's hundred pound*

The bell-founders themselves were not averse to using bells for advertising purposes, and one eighteenth-century firm, Evans & Nott, even went as far as knocking their competitors in their inscriptions. Having to re-cast a bell in 1758 made by their rivals Bilbie & Boosh a few years earlier, this forward-looking firm re-hung the bell with the following inscription:

> *Bilbie and Boosh may come and see*
> *What Evans and Nott have done by me!*

As so often happens when philanthropists decide to assist a deserving cause, the actual cost, in the event, has to be kept as low as possible. The cost of a bell is in proportion to the amount of metal used in it, and this, in turn, affects the sound—the greater the mass of metal the deeper the note. One can only have sympathy for the hard-working organiser of a subscription fund for new bells at Glastonbury in 1776 when he caused one of them to bear the rather pointed legend:

> *Our tones would all have been much deeper*
> *If contributions had been greater.*

But most bells, particularly the tenor, express more solemn sentiments, like Amersham's *Unto the Church I do you call, Death to the grave will summon all* (1745). The smallest bell, the treble, often had an inscription in lighter vein, as at Penn, Bucks: *I as trebell doe begin.* But for sheer high spirits it is difficult to beat the wording on the treble at Northenden, Lancs: *Here goes, my brave boys.* Who could ring badly with a bell like that?

Bell stamp of Robert Mot, Whitechapel Bell Foundry (1570).

5. Outings, accidents and odds-and-ends

Because ringing is a hobby that cannot be practised in isolation but only in co-operation with others, a well-marked social tradition has developed over the years. In most parishes this is seen at its best in the annual ringing-outing, which usually takes place on a Saturday during summer. The preparation and organisation associated with an outing may have taken most of the winter, and can be a highly frustrating experience for the person responsible. An outing normally consists of an all-day tour by coach, visiting perhaps half-a-dozen or more towers spread over a wide area and ringing 30 or 40 minutes at each. Usually the towers are a considerable distance away, and the day's trip may well cover a total of 200 miles or more. The towers chosen must be booked well in advance through the vicar, who will usually give his approval but pass on the message to the tower captain for details of time of arrival and departure, exact location, and other such matters. Meals have to be organised, comparative menus and prices approved, a coach hired and, with luck, every seat booked and paid for! The frustrations arise when the vicar gives his approval, but forgets to advise the tower captain of the visit. Or again, another band may be visiting the area chosen and may conflict with your itinerary. But after seemingly endless correspondence everything is finally arranged, and all one can do is to hope for fine weather and a good attendance. It is unusual for a tower to have enough ringers to fill a coach, so ringers from other towers are invited and also non-ringers from the parish. Many people who do not ring take the opportunity of enjoying a day away from home and visiting other churches, where they can wander round and explore while the more strenuous members get on with the ringing.

The ringing societies attached to universities and other organisations often have an annual ringing-tour that lasts several days, and really dedicated ringers will devote a week of their summer holiday to the tour. In a few cases there is an annual ringing event at a specific place attended by ringers from far afield. This happens at Appleton, near Oxford, on a day known as 'The Fourth of March' but which takes place usually on the first Saturday of March irrespective of the date. Here the bells of St. Lawrence are available all day, the village inns remain open and the festivities include an enormous supper after the ringing is over. Appleton's celebrations originated over a hundred years ago when new bells were donated. Memories are long in Oxfordshire!

The reasons for ringing peals

In the pages of *The Ringing World* one may find accounts of ringing-outings and tours during the last fifty years. The journal's main function, however, is to record peals and quarter-peals successfully rung, and these are listed under county or diocesan guild and arranged according to the number of bells in the method. The name of the ringer of each bell is given, and there is very often a foot-note giving the reason why the peal was rung. It may be in honour of a ringer's 21st birthday; to celebrate the engagement or marriage of ringers; to welcome a new incumbent or to commemorate a church feast. Ringers have not changed a great deal over the years, and it must be admitted that often the decision is made to 'go for a peal' and the reason for ringing it decided afterwards! Some of the reasons printed in *The Ringing World* seem a little removed from reality and have sparked off acrimonious correspondence on more than one occasion. A good example of this occurred in January 1960, when a peal of *Superlative Surprise Major* was rung at Rothwell, Northants, '. . . to commemorate the hundredth anniversary of the return of Fyodor Dostoyevsky to St. Petersburg aften ten years' exile in Siberia'. Several weeks later correspondence was still continuing as to whether or not the Russian writer could be accurately described as a 'revolutionary' in view of the fact that he died in 1881, nearly forty years before the 1917 revolution. The question whether this constituted a valid reason for ringing a peal had obviously long been forgotten.

Sometimes a peal is rung which consists of ringers all with the same Christian name or, more rarely, with the same surname. Ringing certainly seems to go in families, and to continue from one generation to another, though few can beat the record of the Truss family of Marlow who are mentioned in the parish records as ringers in 1593 and whose descendants were still ringing in 1893, and probably after that! Forty years seem a short span in comparison with three hundred, but are an impressive period for continued ringing. In Buckinghamshire, where ringing seems to act as a preservative, the six sons of Robert Gibbs of Winslow rang in the New Year together forty times in succession during the eighteenth century.

Another 'record' peal was achieved in 1952, when, after one or two abortive attempts, a peal was rung at St. John the Evangelist, Deptford, by eight ringers all over eighty years of age!

A peal for such a purpose, even though not a religious one, may be allowed with more logic than that for Dostoyevsky. Unfortunately many younger ringers become obsessed by numbers, and quantity rather than quality becomes their aim. This leads to the pernicious practice known as 'tower-grabbing' in which a small band of ringers tours a district without previous arrangement or warning and tries to ring in as many towers as they can 'grab' during the day. Occasionally there is news of bands attempting to ring several peals in one day. As a peal takes rather more than three hours to ring, one must salute the ringers of Hereford for their brawn, if not for their brain, in ringing five peals in one day including one which had to be re-started after 40 minutes' ringing.

Mishaps and dangers

Though ringing for sixteen hours of the twenty-four may infuriate local residents and make them unsympathetic to ringers, there is usually little harm done to either bells or ringers. An exception to this took place at Liverpool in 1810 when, during Sunday morning ringing, the tower, belfry and spire began to disintegrate and the ringers only just escaped before the whole steeple came roaring down in a heap of dust and rubble, bringing the bells with it. Accidents during ringing are comparatively rare, and those that do happen usually involve learners. The most common type of mishap is caused by letting a novice practise on a heavy bell before full control has been obtained. The learner, falling into the common error of equating a heavy bell with a massive physical effort, pulls too hard on his rope as the bell nears its maximum swing, the result being that at the next stroke the bell swings too quickly upwards and the stay not only hits the slider but snaps it in two. The bell, with nothing to retain it, swings right over and completes a full circle, at the same time winding the rope up round the wheel. The normal reaction of an inexperienced ringer in such a situation is to hold on to the rope in the hope that the bell can be stopped, but this is unlikely to happen. The rope and sally rise into the air, the ringer clings on tightly and in some cases his head is cracked on the ceiling and he falls unconscious to the floor below, sustaining further injury. Fortunately in most properly conducted towers, the learner is never put on a heavy bell and invariably has an experienced ringer with him all the time until he is proficient in handling his bell. The majority of fatal accidents occur when a keen but misguided non-ringer, perhaps a new curate, decides to explore the belfry and look at the bells between morning and evening service. Before ringing can start, the bells have to be ' rung up' so that each is set ready mouth upwards. This takes time, and it is therefore customary to leave the bells 'up' between services, 'ringing down' after Evensong has ended. Modern bells, mounted on ball-bearings, are surprisingly sensitive and when 'set' can easily be pushed off balance so that they swing down. On occasion even the vibration of passing traffic has caused this. It is obviously extremely dangerous for someone unfamiliar with bells to be moving about immediately underneath a 20-cwt bell when the slightest movement could send it crashing down. Nobody should ever go near the bells when they are 'set', and before ringing starts the captain should check that everyone is present and that nobody is still up in the belfry. This is the reason why most belfry doors are kept locked, as so many accidents have happened this way. But even experienced ringers have come to grief, and in many towers a clearly printed notice is displayed if the tower is vacated and the bells left 'up' drawing attention to the very real dangers involved. That these dangers were recognised even in the early days of change-ringing is shown by one of the Rules at All Saints, Stamford, dated 1694.

> *All you that do intend to ring*
> *You undertake a Dangerous thing.*

Bell stamp of William A. and Douglas Hughes, Whitechapel Bell Foundry (1968).

6. Some notable towers and bells

It is usual to think of the tower and bells as being part of the church building, and attached to it, but this is not always so. In some churches the tower is a separate unit away from the main building. A good example is at St. Michael and All Angels, Ledbury, where a separate bell-tower was built on the north side of the church. Probably the best-known tower standing on its own is at Evesham, Worcestershire, a twelve-bell tower on which many famous peals have been rung. The usual explanation of a separate tower for the bells is that the original structure did not prove strong enough to support their weight, and therefore a specially strengthened tower was built to house them.

In other churches, when this situation arose, it was not thought necessary to build a tower and the bells were accommodated in a 'bell-house' at ground level. A well-known example is at East Bergholt, Suffolk, where the ring of five bells (including a 25 cwt tenor) is in a picturesque timber cage in the churchyard.

Quite apart from the bells and tower being separated from the church another unexpected feature occasionally encountered is the juxtaposition of bells and ringers. At Merton College, Oxford, the ringing chamber is not a chamber at all, but a narrow gallery running round the inside of the tower from which one looks straight down to the chapel floor 60 feet below. The ringers stand two on each side, and the bells are but 20 feet above their heads, making ringing at Merton a frightening but most memorable experience! Any situation where the ropes come down at an angle to the ringer makes things complicated, and at Southwell Cathedral, Notts, there was a gallery similar to that at Merton College but with the additional hazard that the bells were hung anti-clockwise, which meant that when ringing rounds the order of pulling the ropes from treble to tenor was the opposite way round the ringing-chamber from the usual. A floor has now been provided in the ringing-chamber.

Ringing towers

Bell-towers unconnected with any church, and built for the sole purpose of ringing bells, are few in this country. The most famous is the campanile at Taylor's Bell Foundry at Loughborough, which has a ring of ten bells and has been visited by more ringers than any other tower in the country. Another record is held by the clock-tower of Manchester Town Hall which is said to contain more bell-metal than any other belfry in Britain, having a ring of 24 bells with a total weight of 42 tons. Twelve of them are hung for ringing, the remainder are in use as a carillon.

These towers are either municipal or industrial undertakings. But one tower exists, complete with a ring of twelve bells, which was built entirely at the expense of one man for the sole purpose of furthering the art of ringing. This is the Waterloo Tower at Quex Park, near Birchington, Kent, and was built by John Powell, the local squire, in 1819. The tower itself is designed in the 'Gothic' style so dear to nineteenth-century architects, with a curious spire of curly cast iron surmounting the whole. The official description issued at the time explains that the idea of the spire was to make '. . . a noble sea mark, being only one mile from that briny fluid'. The twelve bells were cast by the Whitechapel Bell Foundry, and the official opening in August, 1819, attracted a considerable crowd and both the Cumberland Youths and College Youths took part in the ringing. Quex Park is still a popular rendezvous for ringers and is included in many tours in the south of England.

In the south-east corner of the precincts of Chester Cathedral, by the Cheshire Regiment Memorial Garden, is a free-standing tower or campanile where the cathedral bells are hung. The tower itself is a concrete structure, with brick in-filling and clad with Bethesda slates. It was designed by George Pace and finished in 1974, and is the first free-standing bell-tower built for a cathedral in Britain since the fifteenth century. The bells consist of a ring of twelve and a flat sixth. Each bell is named after a saint, Celtic or Anglo-Saxon, venerated in Chester and its neighbourhood. The tenor bell weighs 24¾ cwt.

Famous bells

One subject always of great interest is the weight of the bells. Here it is important to differentiate between single bells hung for chiming and bells hung for ringing in the way we have described. Bells hung for chiming are not usually mounted on a wheel and can be swung through only a short arc. The short travel of the bell causes the clapper to strike the inside and so sound. Bells hung for ringing are mounted on a wheel and need to be swung mouth upwards for change-ringing to be possible. This obviously limits the weight of bells used for ringing, whereas bells for chiming can be very much heavier.

The heaviest bell in Britain is Great Paul at St Paul's Cathedral, London, which weighs 334 cwt. Needless to say this bell is hung for chiming only, as is Big Ben at Westminster (270 cwt). Other heavy bells for chiming include Great George at the University of Bristol (191 cwt) and Oxford's Great Tom at Christ Church (120 cwt) which still chimes 101 times each evening to call in the original 101 scholars of the college.

The heaviest bell hung for actual ringing is the Emmanuel Bell of Liverpool Cathedral weighing just over 4 tons (82cwt). Next is the tenor of Exeter Cathedral at 72 cwt and the tenor of St Paul's Cathedral, London, weighing 62 cwt. When it is remembered that the weight of the tenor in a six-bell tower in most parish churches is around 13-15 cwt it will be realised that an extremely high standard of ringing is required to control bells of such size and weight. York Minster has a tenor of 59 cwt, and Bristol and Wells bells of 50 and 56¼ cwt respectively. (Wells has the heaviest ring of ten bells in the country.) After St. Paul's, the heaviest ringing bell in London is the tenor at Southwark Cathedral with a weight of 48 cwt, while the heaviest bell in an ordinary London church is 41 cwt at St Michael's, Cornhill. Britain's oldest bell is almost certainly that at Caversfield, Oxon, which, though not dated, can be fairly safely assigned to about the year 1250. Like another ancient bell at Goring-on-Thames dating from 1290 it is no longer rung but preserved on view in the church. Striking or chiming, instead of ringing it in the normal way, tends to shorten the life of a bell. The impact of the hammer is on the same spot each time and is concentrated on a smaller area than happens with a clapper which, in any case, strikes the inside first on one side and then on the other. Even so, church bells do have to have regular attention, and it is customary at intervals of several years to take them down and re-hang them a quarter-circle round so that the clapper strikes at a new place. In extreme cases the bells are melted down in the foundry and, after the required 'topping-up' with extra metal, are re-cast to the same mould. This will often be done if the bell develops a crack, and Great Tom at Oxford was recast at least six times during the eighteenth century. In contrast, Big Ben, installed over a hundred years ago, is also cracked, but nothing has ever been done about it!

Superstitions and regional styles

Needless to say there are many superstitions connected with bells and ringing. Most of them are associated with death and burial, and the Passing Bell and the Nine Tailors are well known. Despite this they are often confused. The Passing Bell should be tolled when a parishioner is dying, the Nine Tailors being rung only when a man finally dies. The name is a corruption from 'tellers', and while nine strokes indicated the death of a man, six were for a woman and three were for the death of a child. From this custom originates the expression 'Nine Tailors make a man'. During the nineteenth century there was a fairly general superstition in rural areas that the soul could not leave the body until the 'tailors' had been rung.

Method-ringing first began in the eastern counties and in London, but oddly enough it is the West Country that has the most bells—and where method-ringing is least popular. Devon has 370 towers where ringing is carried on, Somerset has 328 and Cornwall 146. This compares with only 24 in Northumberland and 90 in Surrey. Though they tend to favour rounds and call-changes in Devon and Cornwall they are extremely proud of their striking, and while a visiting ringer is welcomed most cordially it is much more important that he should strike well than that he be familiar with a large number of complicated methods. It has been known for inexperienced ringers from 'up country' to be slightly condescending to West Country ringers—until they hear them in action and, for the first time, appreciate what perfect striking really means.

Bellringing abroad

For reasons already explained bells hung for ringing in churches overseas are very scarce. Australia has 25 such towers and Canada and the U.S.A. only eight each. Even so, many are unringable through lack of use. One of the most impressive overseas rings to be hung recently is the ten-bell ring at Washington Cathedral. The bells were cast by the Whitechapel Bell Foundry, and the first peal on them was rung by a special band from England on 9th May, 1964. Though Washington Cathedral is designed externally in a surprisingly conventional Gothic style the interior arrangements are certainly modern. The ringing-chamber, reached by a speedy and silent lift, holds many people besides the ringers! The bells forming the carillon were cast by Taylor's of Loughborough.

Bellringing in America has not always been as popular as it was on this occasion. In 1930 a wealthy industrialist, Richard T. Crane, purchased a ring of bells of a total weight of 26 tons from a Russian monastery, and presented them to Harvard University. A Russian accompanied them to America and supervised the installation at Harvard where they were hung for chiming, as they had been in Russia. So enthusiastic was the Russian that once they were installed he insisted on giving a solo performance several times each day, much to the annoyance of the undergraduates. The recitals were eventually terminated in a way only students could have devised. Richard T. Crane, the donor, had made his money from the manufacture of sanitary fittings. One day, the moment ringing started, every student on the premises simultaneously flushed his lavatory cistern, a process which almost literally drowned the bells as it also flooded the entire sewage system!

Present-day ringing in Britain

In Britain ringing is accepted as part of the normal pattern of life, and only occasionally is there opposition. Families with small children living near churches are not usually over-enthusiastic about ringing on practice-nights, which in most towers is once a week and lasts from about 7 p.m. to 9 p.m. But if ringing stops promptly at the agreed time there is usually no trouble and, when all is said and done, the church and bells were there long before the houses.

In some towers where there are only just enough ringers it has become customary to stop ringing during the months of July and August, when holidays reduce the ranks still further. It is curious that the cessation of ringing for a period calls forth much more comment from the public than complaints of too much ringing. As far as the ordinary citizen is concerned he recognises that the bells are ringing, but knows nothing of methods or call-changes nor, as a recent survey has shown, is he too sure how many bells are actually ringing. It seems better, therefore, when some ringers are absent, to ring even only three bells (paying attention to the striking!) rather than to cancel all ringing because there are not enough present to ring a proper method.

The answer to this problem is, of course, the recruitment of more ringers. If you live anywhere near the parish church you will already know which night is practice-night, or you can easily find out. There is nothing at all to stop you going along and asking permission to watch and, if you are interested, the finer points of ringing will be explained to you. You will certainly not be asked to ring, or even to touch a rope, unless you express a wish to learn ringing, though many non-ringers seem to think that they will immediately be given a rope and told to get on with it! The replacement of stays, sliders and ropes is far too costly for that!

The chances are, if you go and watch on practice-nights, that you will want to ring before long. If you do so you will embark on a pursuit of absorbing interest, made more fascinating by the realisation that as long as you ring you will also learn, for you can never possibly know it all. There is the companionship of other ringers, the annual outings, visits to other towers and, at home, the care and attention needed in the belfry to keep the bells in good order. You may well become an enthusiast—and you will have every right to be one. But don't let your enthusiasm blind you to the fact that you are ringing for the church—and for the Glory of God. Having this always in mind will ensure that you derive the maximum satisfaction from a hobby that is comparatively unusual, yet very much part of the fabric of English history.

7. Some common terms in bellringing

Back-stroke   The swing of the bell which allows the minimum length of rope to descend to the ringing-chamber.

Bob   A 'call' by the conductor during change-ringing that causes an odd number of bells to vary their normal pattern of work.
(see Single)

Call-changes   Changes in the order in which the bells ring which occur only when 'called' by the conductor.

Campanology   A word used for bellringing, mainly by those who are not ringers.

Caters   Changes rung on 9 bells. The name is derived from *quattuor* (4) and refers to the fact that 4 pairs of bells are involved at each change.

Change-ringing   A system of ringing which causes a different change to be rung at each pull of the rope.

Course   The work performed by a particular bell during the ringing of a method.

Dodge   A manoeuvre during change-ringing in which two bells change places three times before continuing on their normal path.

Doubles   Methods rung on 5 bells.

Exercise (The)   A word used for bellringing by those who consider themselves experienced ringers and wish this fact to be widely known.

Extent   The maximum number of changes possible on a ring of bells without repetition.

False   Used to denote a composition in ringing in which a change has accidentally been repeated.

Grandsire   One of the earliest systems of change-ringing. It is pronounced 'Grandser'.

Hand-stroke   The opposite swing of the bell from back-stroke, and results in the maximum length of rope being available and enables the ringer to grasp the sally.

Hunting   The unvarying path of one bell, usually the treble, which starts by ringing first and gradually changes to being last (hunting up). The reverse process, from last to first is called 'hunting down'.

Lead   The position of being the first bell to ring in a change.

Major   Methods rung on 8 bells.

Maximus   Methods rung on 12 bells.

Method   A series of changes rung in an order that has been standardised and named and which, because each ringer knows the work of his bell, should be rung without any assistance from the conductor. (At least that's the theory!)

Minimus   Changes rung on 4 bells.

Minor   Methods rung on 6 bells.

Muffled   Bells are muffled for funerals by attaching a leather pad to the clapper to deaden the sound. If a pad is attached to one side only the bells are 'half-muffled', if on both sides then they are 'fully muffled'.

Peal   A series of changes conforming to certain definite rules and consisting of not less than 5,040 changes on 7 bells or a minimum of 5,000 on 8 bells. A peal usually takes about three hours to ring.

Plain Bob   The name given to what is probably the first system of change-ringing invented.

Pricking-out   Writing down each individual change in a method so that the work of each bell can be seen.

Queens A change in which all the odd-numbered bells strike first followed by the even-numbered, viz: 1 3 5 7 2 4 6 8.

Ring The name used to indicate all the bells in a tower, e.g., 'a ring of 6' or 'a ring of 12'. Also used to describe the action of ringing, e,g., 'Did you have a good ring at Twittering Parva?'

Ringing-up Before ringing can commence the bells must be raised from their normal position to being 'set' mouth upwards. This process is called 'ringing up' and entails pulling the bellrope on longer and longer strokes as the bell swings through a wider and wider arc until it performs a complete circle and can be 'set'. At each swing the clapper will be striking the side and the bell will chime first in rapid succession but gradually at an increasing interval until the normal rhythm is reached. Experienced ringers often ring up 'in peal' which means raising each bell at the same time but with such exactitude that the chiming remains regular and distinct, from the rapid sequence at the beginning to the normal striking speed when the bells are finally 'up'. The reverse process is 'ringing down' and here again the striking gets faster and faster as the swing becomes shorter and shorter, but ideally the note of each bell should still be separate and distinct until the ringing stops. In many towers the bells are 'rung up' singly or in pairs.

Rope-sight The art of recognising the position and intended path of the other bells by watching the movement of the respective sallies.

Rounds The ringing of bells in order from treble to tenor.

Royal Methods rung on 10 bells.

Sally A fluffy, striped section of coloured material woven into the bellrope a few feet before the end, which serves as an 'indicator' (see 'Rope-sight') and also allows a better grip.

Setting a bell Pulling the rope hard enough to make the bell swing until it is completely upright, then letting it go just off-balance so that the slider rests against the stay and the bell remains 'up' until the rope is pulled again.

Silent peal   Not what you think! A peal rung without a conductor and without anyone 'calling'.

Single   A 'call' which causes a pair, or other even
(see Bob)   number of bells, to make an alteration in their normal work.

Skeleton course   A way of writing out the changes in a method so that the work of only one bell is shown.

'Stand'   The word shouted by the conductor to stop the bells ringing. It is 'called' at one back-stroke and the bells are 'set' at the next back-stroke. If ringing stops except for one bell which continues to give a solo, this usually means that the ringer is a learner and cannot 'set' his bell at will, or that he is stone-deaf.

Stedman   An early system of change-ringing invented by Fabian Stedman of Cambridge about 1660.

Surprise   The name given to certain methods of unusual complexity.

Tenor   The heaviest bell in a ring, with the deepest tone. Numerically it has the highest number.

Tied bell   A bell in which a piece of wood is wedged each side of the clapper so that it is fixed and cannot sound. Used in teaching learners to handle the bell.

Treble   The smallest and lightest-toned bell. It is usually the first to ring, and as it is pulled 'off' the ringer shouts 'Treble's going — gone' to alert the others.

Triples   Methods rung on 7 bells.

True   The name given to a composition that is not 'false', i.e., it conforms to the rules and no change is repeated.

Whole-pull   The complete swing of the bell first one way then the other, and therefore including both hand-stroke and back-stroke.

Finishing the core of a bell mould with a crook in the 1850s (Whitechapel Bell Foundry).

Further reading

Camp, John. *Bellringing*. David and Charles, 1974.
Camp, John. *In Praise of Bells*. Hale, 1988.
Cattermole, P. *Church Bells and Bellringing*. Boydell and Brewer, 1991.
Crocket, Mary. *Bells in Our Lives*. David and Charles, 1973.
Dove, R. H. *A Bellringer's Guide to the Church Bells and Ringing Peals of the World*. Viggers, 1988.
Ingram, Tom. *Bells in England*. Muller, 1954.
Jennings, Trevor S. *Bellfounding*. Shire, reprinted 1992.
Jennings, Trevor S. *Master of My Art, the Taylor Bellfoundries 1784-1987*. The Bellfoundry Museum, Loughborough, 1987.
Jennings, Trevor S. *The Story of Great Paul*. The Bellfoundry Museum, Loughborough, 1986.
Johnston, R. *An Atlas of Bells*. Blackwells, 1990.
Morris, Ernest. *Bells of All Nations*. Hale, 1951.
Morris, Ernest. *Tintinnabula*. Hale, 1959.
Morris, Ernest. *Towers and Bells of Britain*. Hale, 1955.
Nichols, J. R. *Bells thro' the Ages*. Chapman and Hall, 1937.
Price, Percival. *Bells and Man*. Oxford University Press, 1983.
Raven, J. J. *The Bells of England*. Methuen, 1906.
Yolen, Jane. *Ring Out — A Book of Bells*. Evans, 1978.

Places to visit

The Bellfoundry Museum, Freehold Street, Loughborough, Leicestershire LE11 1AR. Telephone: 0509 233414.
Dorset County Museum, High West Street, Dorchester, Dorset DT1 1XA. Telephone: 0305 262735.
Guildford Museum, Castle Arch, Quarry Street, Guildford, Surrey GU1 3SX. Telephone: 0483 444750.
Salisbury and South Wiltshire Museum, The King's House, 65 The Close, Salisbury, Wiltshire SP1 2EN. Telephone: 0722 332151.

Index